Faithful in the Flesh: Living the True Gospel

Apostle Bill Amor

FAITHFUL IN THE FLESH: LIVING THE TRUE GOSPEL
written by Bill Amor
1st Edition © 2025 by Bill Amor
ISBN: 979-8-9995696-6-0

Scripture quotations taken from the KING JAMES VERSION (KJV): KING JAMES VERSION, public domain.

Scripture quotations taken from the Amplified® Bible, Copyright © 1954, 1958, 1962, 1964, 1965, 1987 by The Lockman Foundation. Used by permission. All rights reserved

Index of Chapters

**Summary: Faithful in Flesh: Living the True Gospel"
by Apostle Bill Amor emphasizes the necessity of living a life rooted in faith in Jesus Christ, who came in the flesh. The book explores how true faith manifests through obedience, reliance on God's Word, and rejecting superficial practices that do not align with the Gospel. It challenges readers to examine their lives, ensuring their actions reflect genuine faith and devotion to Christ as their Savior. The central message is that salvation and righteousness come through faith alone, not external rituals or appearances.**

Introduction: In a world filled with distractions, misconceptions, and competing ideologies, the essence of the Gospel often becomes clouded. Many believers struggle to reconcile their faith with the realities of living in a fallen world. What does it truly mean to live faithfully in the flesh while walking by the Spirit? How can we embody the teachings of Jesus Christ in our daily lives without succumbing to legalism or worldly desires? These are questions that lie at the heart of this book.

"Faithful in Flesh: Living the True Gospel" is a journey into understanding and applying the transformative power of faith in Jesus Christ. Rooted deeply in Scripture, this book explores how Jesus, fully God and fully man, became flesh to dwell among us and offer salvation through grace. It challenges readers to examine their lives through the lens of faith and encourages them to live not by their own strength but by reliance on Christ's finished work on the cross.

The chapters ahead will guide you through key themes central to living out your faith:

- **Understanding the Incarnation**: Why did God choose to become flesh? What does this mean for us as believers?

- **Living by Faith**: How do we walk by faith and not by sight, overcoming sin and temptation?

- **The War Within**: A deep dive into the ongoing battle between spirit and flesh.

- **Freedom in Christ**: Discovering what it means to live free from legalism while embracing God's grace.

- **Bearing Fruit Through Abiding in Christ**: How can we produce lasting spiritual fruit by staying connected to Jesus?

- **Crucifying the Flesh**: Practical steps for surrendering sinful desires and living victoriously through faith.

- **Eternal Life Through Faith**: Understanding God's promise of eternal life and how it shapes our present reality.

This book is not merely an academic exploration; it is a call to action. It invites you into a deeper relationship with Jesus Christ—a relationship marked by trust, obedience, and transformation. Whether you are new to Christianity or have been walking with Christ for years, "Faithful in Flesh" offers insights that will challenge you, encourage you, and equip you for faithful discipleship.

As Apostle Paul wrote in Galatians 2:20 (ESV): *"I have been crucified with Christ. It is no longer I who live, but Christ who lives in me. And the life I now live in the flesh I live by faith in the Son of God, who loved me and gave himself for me."* This verse encapsulates what it means to be faithful in flesh—living every moment as a testament to God's love and grace.

Let us embark on this journey together as we seek to understand what it truly means to live out "the true Gospel"—a

Gospel that transforms hearts, renews minds, and empowers us to walk faithfully before our Lord.

Chapter 1: The Word Became Flesh: Understanding the Incarnation

The incarnation of Jesus Christ is one of the most profound and central doctrines of Christianity. It is the belief that God, in His infinite love and wisdom, took on human form in the person of Jesus Christ. This chapter will explore the theological significance, scriptural basis, and practical implications of this cornerstone of Christian faith.

The Meaning of Incarnation

The term "incarnation" comes from the Latin word *incarnatio*, meaning "to make flesh." In Christian theology, it refers to the act by which the eternal Son of God assumed a human nature and became man. This is expressed succinctly in John 1:14: **"The Word became flesh and made his dwelling among us. We have seen his glory, the glory of the one and only Son, who came from the Father, full of grace and truth."**[1]

This verse encapsulates several key truths:

1. **Jesus is fully divine**: The "Word" (Greek: *Logos*) refers to Jesus as preexistent and co-eternal with God (John 1:1).

2. **Jesus is fully human**: By becoming flesh, He entered into human existence with all its limitations—hunger, thirst, fatigue, and even suffering.

3. **Jesus dwelt among us**: The phrase "made his dwelling" literally means "tabernacled" or "pitched His tent," signifying God's presence with humanity.

Scriptural Foundations for the Incarnation

The doctrine of incarnation is not confined to a single verse but is woven throughout Scripture:

- **Philippians 2:6-8** describes how Jesus, though being in very nature God, humbled Himself by taking on human likeness and becoming obedient to death—even death on a cross.

- **Isaiah 7:14** prophesied that a virgin would conceive and bear a son called Immanuel ("God with us"), fulfilled in Matthew 1:23.

- **Hebrews 2:14-17** explains that Jesus shared in our humanity so that He might destroy the power of death and become a merciful high priest.

These passages affirm both Jesus' divinity and humanity—a mystery often referred to as the hypostatic union.

Why Did God Become Flesh?

Understanding why God became flesh requires delving into His redemptive plan for humanity:

1. **To Reveal God to Us**
   In Jesus, we see God's character perfectly revealed (John 14:9). He embodies grace, truth, love, justice, mercy, and holiness.

2. **To Provide an Example for Living**
   As fully human yet without sin (Hebrews 4:15), Jesus serves as our ultimate example for how to live in obedience to God.

3. **To Reconcile Humanity to God**
   Sin created a chasm between humanity and God (Isaiah 59:2). Through His life, death, and resurrection, Jesus bridged this gap (2 Corinthians 5:18-19).

4. **To Defeat Sin and Death**
   By taking on flesh, Jesus could die on behalf of sinners (Romans 5:8) and rise again to conquer death (1 Corinthians 15:54-57).

The Mystery of the Incarnation

While Scripture provides clear teachings about the incarnation's purpose and effects, it remains a profound mystery beyond full human comprehension. How can one person be both fully divine and fully human? Early church councils wrestled with this question:

- The Council of Nicaea (AD 325) affirmed Christ's full divinity.

- The Council of Chalcedon (AD 451) articulated that

Christ has two natures—divine and human—united in one person without confusion or division.

These definitions safeguard against heresies such as Arianism (denying Christ's divinity) or Docetism (denying His humanity).

Practical Implications for Believers

The incarnation has profound implications for how Christians live their faith:

1. **Confidence in God's Love**
   Knowing that God Himself entered into our broken world assures us of His deep love for us.

2. **Hope Amid Suffering**
   Because Jesus experienced pain, rejection, and loss firsthand, He can empathize with our struggles (Hebrews 4:15).

3. **A Call to Humility**
   Just as Christ humbled Himself by becoming human (Philippians 2:5-8), we are called to live humbly before others.

4. **Empowered Living Through Grace**
   The same power that enabled Jesus' earthly ministry now works within believers through the Holy Spirit.

Conclusion

The incarnation is not merely a theological concept but a transformative reality that shapes every aspect of Christian life. It reveals God's heart for humanity while providing hope for redemption and restoration. As we contemplate this great mystery—that "the Word became flesh" we are invited into deeper worship and greater devotion to our Savior.

Chapter 2: Faith in Action: Living by the Spirit, Not the Flesh

Living a life of faith is one of the central tenets of Christianity. It is not merely about professing belief in Jesus Christ but also about allowing that faith to transform every aspect of one's life. This transformation involves a shift from living according to the desires of the flesh to living by the guidance and power of the Holy Spirit. In this chapter, we will explore what it means to live by the Spirit, why it is essential for a faithful Christian life, and how believers can practically apply this principle in their daily walk with God.

Understanding "The Flesh" and "The Spirit"

To understand what it means to live by the Spirit, we must first define "the flesh" and "the Spirit" as they are used in Scripture. The term "flesh" (Greek: *sarx*) often refers to human nature in its fallen state—our sinful tendencies and desires that are opposed to God's will. The Apostle Paul describes these works of the flesh in Galatians 5:19-21, which include sexual immorality, idolatry, jealousy, fits of anger, selfish ambition, envy, drunkenness, and other similar behaviors.

In contrast, "the Spirit" refers to the Holy Spirit—the third person of the Trinity—who indwells believers and empowers them to live according to God's will. When someone becomes a follower of Christ, they receive the Holy Spirit as a gift (Acts 2:38). The Spirit enables Christians to overcome sin and produce godly characteristics known as the fruit of the Spirit: love, joy, peace, patience, kindness, goodness, faithfulness, gentleness, and self-control (Galatians 5:22-23).

Why Living by the Spirit Matters

Living by the Spirit is not optional for Christians; it is essential for experiencing true freedom in Christ. Paul writes in Romans 8:1-2 that "there is now no condemnation for those who are in Christ Jesus because through Christ Jesus the law of the Spirit who gives life has set you free from the law of sin and death." This freedom does not mean indulging sinful desires but rather being liberated from their control.

When believers walk by the Spirit:

1. **They Fulfill God's Law:** Paul explains that love fulfills all commandments (Romans 13:10), and love is a fruit produced by walking in step with the Spirit.

2. **They Experience Transformation:** As Christians yield to God's work within them through His Spirit (2 Corinthians 3:18), they are transformed into Christ's likeness.

3. **They Bear Witness:** A life led by God's Spirit serves as a testimony to others about His power and grace.

Practical Steps for Living by Faith Through the Holy Spirit

1. **Daily Surrender:** Begin each day with prayerfully surrendering your plans and desires to God. Ask Him for guidance through His Word and His Holy Spirit.

2. **Meditate on Scripture:** The Bible reveals God's character and will for our lives. Regularly reading and meditating on Scripture helps believers align their thoughts with God's truth (Psalm 119:105).

3. **Cultivate Spiritual Disciplines:** Practices such as prayer, fasting, worshipping with other believers, serving others selflessly—all help nurture dependence on God rather than reliance on oneself.

4. **Be Mindful of Your Thoughts:** Take every thought captive under obedience unto Christ (2 Corinthians10 :5)

Conclusion

In conclusion, living by the Spirit and not by the flesh is a transformative journey that requires a steadfast commitment to faith in Jesus Christ. The flesh represents our natural inclinations, often driven by selfish desires and worldly temptations, while the Spirit calls us to a higher standard of living rooted in love, joy, peace, patience, kindness, goodness, faithfulness, gentleness, and self-control (Galatians

5:22-23). By surrendering to the guidance of the Holy Spirit, believers are empowered to overcome sin and live lives that reflect God's righteousness.

Faith in action is not merely about external behaviors or adherence to religious rituals; it is about an internal transformation that manifests outwardly through acts of love and obedience to God's will. This chapter has emphasized that true faith produces fruit—visible evidence of a life aligned with God's purposes. As James 2:26 reminds us, "Faith without works is dead," underscoring that genuine faith must be accompanied by actions inspired by the Spirit.

Ultimately, living by the Spirit enables believers to experience freedom from the bondage of sin and legalism. It allows them to walk confidently in their identity as children of God, fully assured of His grace and mercy. This path requires daily reliance on prayer, Scripture study, and fellowship with other believers to remain attuned to the Spirit's leading. Through this faithful pursuit, Christians can fulfill their calling to be ambassadors of Christ in a broken world.

May this chapter inspire readers to embrace a life led by the Spirit—a life marked not by perfection but by continual growth in faith and obedience. In doing so, they will glorify God and bear witness to His transformative power at work within them.

Chapter 3: The True Gospel: Grace and Truth Through Jesus Christ

The concept of the "True Gospel" is deeply rooted in the teachings of the New Testament, particularly in the Gospel of John. This chapter explores how grace and truth are revealed through Jesus Christ, focusing on key passages from John 1 and John 3.

The Word Became Flesh: A Revelation of Grace and Truth (John 1:14-18)

In John 1:14, it is written: *"The Word became flesh and made his dwelling among us. We have seen his glory, the glory of the one and only Son, who came from the Father, full of grace and truth."* This verse encapsulates one of the most profound truths of Christianity—the incarnation. The eternal Word (Logos), which was with God and was God (John 1:1), took on human form to dwell among humanity. This act signifies God's ultimate expression of love and humility.

The phrase "full of grace and truth" highlights two essential attributes that Jesus embodies:

- **Grace** refers to God's unmerited favor toward humanity. Through Jesus, this grace is extended to all people, offering forgiveness for sins and reconciliation with God.

- **Truth** represents God's faithfulness to His promises and the revelation of His divine nature. In Jesus, we see the perfect embodiment of God's truth—He is both the messenger and the message.

John 1:16-17 further elaborates on this theme: *"Out of his fullness we have all received grace in place of grace already given. For the law was given through Moses; grace and truth came through Jesus Christ."* Here, John contrasts the old covenant under Moses with the new covenant established by Jesus. While the Law revealed God's standards for righteousness, it could not provide salvation. In contrast, Jesus brings a new era where grace abounds, enabling believers to experience a personal relationship with God.

The Necessity of Faith in Jesus (John 3:16-21)

John 3 contains one of the most well-known verses in Scripture—John 3:16: *"For God so loved the world that he gave his one and only Son, that whoever believes in him shall not perish but have eternal life."* This verse succinctly captures the essence of the Gospel:

- **God's Love:** The motivation behind sending Jesus was God's immense love for humanity.

- **Jesus' Sacrifice:** By giving His "one and only Son," God provided a way for sinners to be redeemed.

- **Faith as a Requirement:** Eternal life is promised to those who believe in Jesus.

This passage also emphasizes that salvation is not earned through works or adherence to religious rituals but is a gift received through faith. As stated in John 3:17, *"For God did not send his Son into the world to condemn the world, but to save the world through him."* The purpose of Jesus' mission was redemptive—to rescue humanity from sin rather than to judge it.

However, John 3:18-21 introduces an important distinction between those who accept this gift and those who reject it:

- Those who believe in Jesus are not condemned because their faith aligns them with God's plan for salvation.

- Those who do not believe stand condemned already because they have rejected God's provision for their redemption.

The imagery of light versus darkness in John 3:19-21 further illustrates this point. Jesus is described as "the light" that has come into the world. People who love truth come into this light so that their deeds may be exposed as being done in God. Conversely, those who prefer darkness avoid coming into this light because they fear their evil deeds will be exposed.

Grace That Transforms Lives

The true Gospel does more than offer forgiveness—it transforms lives by bringing people into a relationship with God through faith in Jesus Christ. As recipients of grace:

1. Believers are empowered to live according to God's will rather than being enslaved by sin (Romans 6:14).

2. They are called to extend grace toward others as an expression of gratitude for what they have received (Ephesians 4:32).

3. They walk in truth by aligning their lives with God's Word (John 17:17).

In conclusion, **the true Gospel reveals both God's boundless grace and His unwavering truth through Jesus Christ**. It invites all people to respond in faith so they may experience eternal life—a life marked by freedom from sin's power and fellowship with their Creator.

Apostle Bill Amor, a follower (not sent by people or through people, but by Jesus Christ—the Savior—and God the Father, who raised Him from the dead), and all those reborn in the Spirit of Jesus—the few predestined and chosen fathers, mothers, brothers, and sisters with me:

To the few chosen born-again members of Christ's Body (and we pray—not for worldly churches that follow human rules and love this wicked world; we leave them alone):

Grace and peace—calmness and spiritual health—to

you from God our Father and the Lord Jesus Christ, who gave Himself to cleanse us from our sins...to save us and purify us from all unrighteousness...so He might rescue us from this evil age, according to the will and plan of our God and Father. To Him be ALL glory forever and ever. Amen.

Believers, the good news we proclaim is not a human invention. It is not derived from people, nor was it taught to us by anyone; instead, it was revealed directly by Jesus Christ, who lives eternally in His risen body.

I am astonished and deeply troubled that some of you are so quickly deserting Him who called you by the grace of Christ for a different gospel—though there is no other true gospel. There are some who are troubling you and distorting the gospel of Christ into something false. But even if we or an angel from heaven should preach a gospel contrary to what we originally proclaimed to you, let them be accursed! As I have said before, I now repeat: If anyone preaches a gospel different from what you received from us, let them be accursed!

I thank You, Father, Lord of heaven and earth, for hiding these truths from the so-called wise and learned and revealing them to the humble and childlike. Yes, Father, for this was Your good pleasure.

In the beginning was the Word, and the Word was with God, and the Word was God. He was with God in the beginning. Through Him all things were made; without

Him nothing was made that has been made.

In Him was life, and that life was the light of all mankind. The light shines in the darkness, but the darkness has not understood it.

He came to His own people, but His own did not receive Him. Yet to all who did receive Him, to those who believed in His name, He gave the right to become children of God—children born not of natural descent, nor of human decision or a husband's will, but born of God's Spirit.

We call on you today because Jesus sent us to proclaim: "You must be born again! You must be born again!" For those who are born again are invited to go deeper into resting fully in Him and relying on His grace.

Jesus desires to give you a fresh start today—a new beginning. Today is your opportunity! You've heard this message before:

"For God so loved the world that He gave His one and only Son, that whoever believes in Him shall not perish but have eternal life."

Those who believe this truth embrace eternal life and

enter Heaven...but those who reject it or hesitate turn away from their rescue into God's Kingdom. They resist His invitation and choose their own path toward eternal separation—Hell—an everlasting loss.

Ultimately, it comes down to your choice: God will not judge you based on your deeds alone but will ask one question: "What did you do with My Son Jesus Christ?"

Jesus Himself declared: "Come to Me, all you who are weary and burdened, and I will give you rest." (Matthew 11:28)

Jesus desires to lift you from wherever you are and bring you into His Kingdom, offering a life filled with purpose here on Earth and eternal joy in Heaven!

This is about experiencing **the fullness of life now** and the promise of **eternal life forever.**

Your time on Earth is fleeting—a mere moment compared to eternity. **Choose today whom you will follow!** Come to Jesus now; today is your opportunity to be saved from condemnation and shame.

You cannot change the past, and tomorrow is uncertain. **But today is the day for salvation. Act now while there's still time.**

Life is fragile—we've all seen people here one moment and gone the next. Don't wait until it's too late.

Call on the name of Jesus Christ today while the door remains open. There is no other name under heaven or on Earth by which we can be saved but the name of Jesus Christ.

Call on Him today, and may God bless you abundantly!

Chapter 4: Walking by Faith: Overcoming Sin in the Flesh

The concept of walking by faith is central to Christian theology and practice. It is rooted in the belief that faith in Jesus Christ enables believers to overcome sin and live a life pleasing to God. This chapter explores the biblical foundation for walking by faith, the relationship between faith and sin, and practical steps for overcoming sin through a life of faith.

The Biblical Foundation for Walking by Faith

The Bible emphasizes the importance of faith as the cornerstone of a believer's relationship with God. In 2 Corinthians 5:7, Paul writes, "For we walk by faith, not by sight." This verse underscores that Christians are called to live their lives based on trust in God's promises rather than relying solely on their own understanding or sensory experiences. Faith is not merely intellectual assent but an active trust in God's character, His Word, and His redemptive work through Jesus Christ.

Hebrews 11 provides numerous examples of individuals who walked by faith, such as Abraham, Moses, and Noah. These men and women trusted God even when His plans seemed impossible or incomprehensible. Their lives demonstrate that walking by faith requires obedience, perseverance, and reliance on God's strength rather than human effort.

The Relationship Between Faith and Sin

The Bible teaches that anything done without faith is sin. Romans 14:23 states, "But whoever has doubts is condemned if they eat, because their eating is not from faith; and everything that does not come from faith is sin." This verse highlights the principle that actions disconnected from trust in God are inherently sinful because they stem from self-reliance or unbelief.

Sin originates from a lack of faith in God's goodness and sufficiency. In Genesis 3, Adam and Eve's disobedience was rooted in their doubt about God's command and His intentions for them. Similarly, when believers act out of fear, pride, or selfish ambition rather than trusting God's guidance, they fall into sin.

Faith empowers believers to overcome sin by aligning their hearts with God's will. Galatians 5:16-17 explains this dynamic: "So I say, walk by the Spirit, and you will not gratify the desires of the flesh. For the flesh desires what is contrary to the Spirit, and the Spirit what is contrary to the flesh." Walking by faith involves yielding to the Holy Spirit's leading rather than succumbing to sinful impulses.

Practical Steps for Walking by Faith

1. **Cultivate a Deep Relationship with God**
   Walking by faith begins with knowing God intimately through prayer, worship, and studying Scripture. As believers grow in their understanding of God's char-

acter and promises, their trust in Him deepens.

2. **Renew Your Mind**
Romans 12:2 encourages believers to be transformed by renewing their minds. This involves replacing worldly thinking with biblical truth. Meditating on verses like Philippians 4:13 ("I can do all things through Christ who strengthens me") reinforces confidence in God's power to overcome sin.

3. **Depend on the Holy Spirit**
The Holy Spirit plays a crucial role in enabling believers to walk by faith. Galatians 5:22-23 describes the fruit of the Spirit—qualities like love, joy, peace, patience—that counteract sinful tendencies. By seeking the Spirit's guidance daily, Christians can resist temptation and live victoriously.

4. **Confess Sin Regularly**
Acknowledging areas where one has fallen short fosters humility and dependence on God's grace. First John 1:9 assures believers that if they confess their sins, God is faithful to forgive them and purify them from unrighteousness.

5. **Surround Yourself with Fellow Believers**
Community is vital for spiritual growth. Hebrews 10:24-25 urges Christians to encourage one another toward love and good deeds while meeting together regularly for fellowship.

6. **Actively Trust God in Every Situation**
Walking by faith means choosing trust over fear or doubt regardless of circumstances (Proverbs 3:5-6). Whether facing trials or making decisions about daily

life matters like finances or relationships—faithful reliance on God leads away from sinful choices toward righteousness.

Conclusion

Walking by faith transforms every aspect of a believer's life—from overcoming personal struggles with sin to fulfilling God's purposes here on earth faithfully until eternity comes into view fully realized! By trusting wholly upon Christ's finished work at Calvary coupled alongside active participation empowered via indwelling presence Holy Ghost within us daily—we find ourselves equipped more than conquerors able stand firm midst adversities temptations alike!

Chapter 5: The War Within: Spirit Versus Flesh

The struggle between the spirit and the flesh is a central theme in Christian theology, deeply rooted in biblical teachings. This internal conflict is described vividly in the Bible, particularly in the writings of the Apostle Paul. In this chapter, we will explore what it means to live with this tension, how it manifests in daily life, and how believers can overcome the desires of the flesh through faith and reliance on the Holy Spirit.

Understanding the Conflict

The Bible teaches that humanity is composed of both a physical body (the "flesh") and a spiritual nature. The "flesh" often symbolizes human weakness, sinful tendencies, and desires that are contrary to God's will. In contrast, the "spirit" represents the renewed nature of a believer who has been transformed by faith in Jesus Christ.

Paul addresses this dichotomy explicitly in **Galatians 5:16-17**, where he writes:

"So, I say, walk by the Spirit, and you will not gratify the desires of the flesh. For the flesh desires what is contrary to the Spirit, and the Spirit what is contrary to the flesh. They are in conflict with each other so that you are not to do whatever you want."[1]

This passage highlights that there is an ongoing battle within every believer. The flesh pulls us toward sin—toward selfishness, pride, lust, anger, and other destructive behaviors—while the Spirit leads us toward righteousness, love, humility, and obedience to God.

Biblical Examples of This Struggle

The Bible provides numerous examples of individuals wrestling with this internal war:

1. **Adam and Eve**: The first humans succumbed to their fleshly desire for knowledge and power when they disobeyed God by eating from the forbidden tree (Genesis 3). Their choice illustrates how yielding to fleshly desires leads to separation from God.

2. **King David**: Despite being a man after God's own heart (1 Samuel 13:14), David fell into sin when he gave in to his lust for Bathsheba (2 Samuel 11). His story serves as a reminder that even those who are close to God can struggle with their flesh.

3. **Paul's Personal Struggle**: In **Romans 7:15-25**, Paul candidly describes his own battle with sin: *"I do not understand what I do. For what I want to do I do not do, but what I hate I do... For in my inner being I delight in God's law; but I see another law at work in me, waging war against the law of my mind and making me a prisoner of the law of sin at work within me."*[2]

Paul's transparency about his struggles resonates with believers today who face similar challenges.

The Works of the Flesh Versus Fruit of the Spirit

In Galatians 5:19-23, Paul contrasts two opposing forces at work within us:

- **The Works of the Flesh**: These include sexual immorality, impurity, idolatry, hatred, jealousy, fits of rage, selfish ambition, dissensions, envy, drunkenness, and more.

- **The Fruit of the Spirit**: These are love, joy, peace, patience (forbearance), kindness, goodness, faithfulness, gentleness, and self-control.

Paul emphasizes that those who belong to Christ have crucified their sinful nature along with its passions and desires (**Galatians 5:24**) but must continually choose to live by the Spirit.

Overcoming Through Faith

Victory over this internal war is possible only through faith in Jesus Christ and reliance on His power. Here are key principles for overcoming:

1. **Walk by Faith**: Trusting God's promises enables believers to resist temptation. Hebrews 11 provides

examples of individuals who overcame challenges through faith.

2. **Rely on God's Strength**: Philippians 4:13 reminds us that we can do all things through Christ who strengthens us.

3. **Renew Your Mind**: Romans 12:2 urges believers not to conform to worldly patterns but be transformed by renewing their minds through Scripture.

4. **Put on Spiritual Armor**: Ephesians 6 describes spiritual armor—truth, righteousness, faith—that equips believers for battle against sin.

5. **Confess Sin Quickly**: When we fail—and we will—we must confess our sins immediately (1 John 1:9) rather than allowing guilt or shame to separate us from God.

Living Victoriously

Living victoriously does not mean perfection but persistence. It involves daily surrendering our lives to Christ and allowing His Spirit to guide our thoughts and actions.

As Paul writes in Galatians 2:20: *"I have been crucified with*

Christ; it is no longer I who live but Christ lives in me; and the life which I now live in the flesh I live by faith in the Son of God."[3]

This verse encapsulates what it means for believers to triumph over their sinful nature—not through their own strength but through Christ living within them.

Conclusion

The war within—the struggle between spirit and flesh—is an inevitable part of every believer's journey. However, daunting it may seem at times; victory is assured for those who place their trust fully in Jesus Christ. By walking daily with Him through prayerful dependence on His Word & Holy-Spirit guidance –we can overcome temptations while bearing fruits pleasing unto Lord!

Chapter 6: Freedom in Christ: No Longer Under the Law

The concept of freedom in Christ is one of the most profound and liberating truths found in the Bible. It is a cornerstone of Christian theology, emphasizing that believers are no longer bound by the Old Testament law but are instead called to live under the grace provided through Jesus Christ. This chapter will explore this theme in detail, drawing from key biblical passages and theological insights to provide a comprehensive understanding of what it means to be free in Christ.

The Law and Its Purpose

To understand freedom in Christ, it is essential first to grasp the purpose of the law. The Apostle Paul explains in Galatians 3:24-25 that "the law was our guardian until Christ came that we might be justified by faith. Now that this faith has come, we are no longer under a guardian." The law served as a tutor or guide, revealing humanity's sinfulness and need for a Savior. It was never intended to provide salvation but rather to point people toward their inability to achieve righteousness on their own.

Romans 3:20 reinforces this idea: "Therefore no one will be declared righteous in God's sight by the works of the law; rather, through the law we become conscious of our sin." The law exposes sin but cannot cleanse it. Its role was preparatory, setting the stage for the coming of Jesus Christ.

Fulfillment of the Law Through Christ

Jesus Himself declared in Matthew 5:17, "Do not think that I have come to abolish the Law or the Prophets; I have not come to abolish them but to fulfill them." By living a sinless life and offering Himself as a perfect sacrifice for sin, Jesus fulfilled all the requirements of the law. His death and resurrection marked the end of humanity's obligation to adhere to ceremonial and sacrificial laws as a means of attaining righteousness.

Hebrews 10:1-4 elaborates on this point, explaining that "the law is only a shadow of the good things that are coming—not the realities themselves." The sacrifices prescribed by the law were insufficient because they could not permanently remove sin. In contrast, Jesus' sacrifice was once for all (Hebrews 10:10), providing complete atonement for those who believe.

Freedom From Legalism

One of Paul's most passionate arguments against legalism is found in Galatians 5:1: "It is for freedom that Christ has set us free. Stand firm, then, and do not let yourselves be burdened again by a yoke of slavery." Here, Paul warns against returning to a system where adherence to rules becomes more important than faith in Christ. Legalism enslaves individuals by creating an impossible standard and fostering guilt when perfection cannot be achieved.

Colossians 2:13-14 further illustrates this freedom: "When

you were dead in your sins... God made you alive with Christ. He forgave us all our sins, having canceled the charge of our legal indebtedness... nailing it to the cross." Believers are no longer judged based on their ability to keep every aspect of Mosaic law because Jesus has already paid their debt.

Living Under Grace

Freedom from the law does not mean believers are free to live however they please. Instead, they are called to live under grace—a higher standard motivated by love rather than obligation. Romans 6:14 states, "For sin shall no longer be your master because you are not under the law but under grace."

This new way of living involves being led by the Holy Spirit (Galatians 5:16-18). The Spirit empowers believers to produce fruit such as love, joy, peace, patience, kindness, goodness, faithfulness, gentleness, and self-control (Galatians 5:22-23). These qualities fulfill God's moral standards without reliance on rigid rules.

Freedom That Leads To Service

Christian freedom is not about self-indulgence but about serving others out of love. Galatians 5:13 exhorts believers: "You... were called to be free. But do not use your freedom to indulge the flesh; rather serve one another humbly in love." True freedom enables Christians to focus outwardly—

loving God wholeheartedly and loving neighbors as themselves (Matthew 22:37-39).

Paul exemplifies this attitude in his ministry when he says in 1 Corinthians 9:19-23 that he became "all things to all people" so that he might save some. His actions demonstrate how freedom can be used responsibly—to advance God's kingdom rather than pursue selfish desires.

Conclusion

Freedom in Christ represents liberation from both sin's power and legalistic bondage while ushering believers into a life characterized by grace-filled obedience and Spirit-led service. This freedom does not negate moral responsibility but transforms it into an expression of gratitude for what Jesus has accomplished on behalf of humanity.

As Paul writes poignantly in Romans 8:1-2: "Therefore there is now no condemnation for those who are in Christ Jesus because through Christ Jesus... [we] have been set free from [the] law... [and] death." Embracing this truth allows Christians everywhere not only peace with God but also purposeful lives dedicated wholly unto Him.

Chapter 7: Love as Fulfillment of the Law: A Life Led by the Spirit

The concept of love as the fulfillment of the law is a central theme in Christian theology, rooted deeply in Scripture. This chapter explores how love, guided by the Holy Spirit, serves as the ultimate expression of obedience to God's commandments and reflects a life transformed by faith in Jesus Christ.

The Biblical Foundation for Love as Fulfillment of the Law

The Apostle Paul explicitly states in Romans 13:8-10 that love fulfills the law. He writes:

"Owe no one anything, except to love each other, for the one who loves another has fulfilled the law. For the commandments, 'You shall not commit adultery, You shall not murder, You shall not steal, You shall not covet,' and any other commandment, are summed up in this word: 'You shall love your neighbor as yourself.' Love does no wrong to a neighbor; therefore, love is the fulfilling of the law." (Romans 13:8-10 ESV) [1]

This passage highlights that all moral obligations outlined in God's law can be distilled into one overarching principle: love. When we act out of genuine love for others, we naturally avoid actions that harm them or violate God's commandments.

Jesus Himself affirmed this truth during His earthly ministry. When asked about the greatest commandment in the Law, He replied:

"'You shall love the Lord your God with all your heart and with all your soul and with all your mind.' This is the great and first commandment. And a second is like it: 'You shall love your neighbor as yourself.' On these two command-ments depend all the Law and the Prophets." (Matthew 22:37-40 ESV) [2]

Here, Jesus emphasizes that loving God wholeheartedly and loving others selflessly encapsulates everything re-quired by God's moral law.

The Role of the Holy Spirit in Leading a Life of Love

While understanding that love fulfills the law is essential, living out this truth requires divine empowerment. Human nature, corrupted by sin, struggles to consistently exhibit selfless love. This is where the Holy Spirit plays a transfor-mative role.

Paul explains in Galatians 5:16-25 that walking by the Spirit enables believers to overcome sinful desires and bear fruit consistent with God's character:

"But I say, walk by the Spirit, and you will not gratify the desires of the flesh... But if you are led by the Spirit, you are not under the law... But the fruit of the Spirit is love, joy, peace, patience, kindness, goodness, faithfulness, gentleness, self-control; against such things there is no law." (Galatians 5:16-23 ESV) [3]

The first fruit listed—love—is foundational because it encompasses all other virtues. A life led by the Spirit produces genuine love for God and others that transcends human effort or obligation.

Practical Expressions of Love Guided by Faith

Living out love as fulfillment of God's law involves practical actions inspired by faith and empowered by grace. Some examples include:

1. **Forgiving Others:** Just as Christ forgave us (Ephesians 4:32), we are called to extend forgiveness even when it feels undeserved.

2. **Serving Selflessly:** Jesus modeled servant leadership when He washed His disciples' feet (John 13:12-17). We reflect His humility when we prioritize others' needs over our own.

3. **Caring for Those in Need:** James reminds us that true religion involves caring for orphans and widows

(James 1:27). Acts of compassion demonstrate Christlike love.

4. **Speaking Truth in Love:** While honesty is vital (Ephesians 4:15), it must always be tempered with kindness and respect.

5. **Loving Enemies:** Perhaps most challenging is Jesus' command to love our enemies and pray for those who persecute us (Matthew 5:44). Such radical love testifies to God's transformative power.

The Eternal Significance of Living a Life Led by Love

Paul underscores in 1 Corinthians 13 that without love—even extraordinary spiritual gifts or sacrificial acts are meaningless:

"If I speak in tongues of men and angels but have not love... I am nothing... So now faith, hope & love abide these three but greatest LOVE"

Was Love When Jesus Said the Woes?

In Matthew Chapter 23, Jesus delivers a series of strong rebukes to the scribes and Pharisees, often referred to as the "Seven Woes." These statements are direct and confrontational, addressing the hypocrisy, legalism, and spiritual blindness of these religious leaders. At first glance, these words may seem harsh or unloving. However, when exam-

ined in the broader context of Jesus' ministry and teachings, it becomes clear that even these stern warnings were
rooted in love.

The Context of Matthew 23

Matthew 23 is a chapter where Jesus openly criticizes
the religious leaders for their hypocrisy and failure to lead
people toward God. He accuses them of burdening others
with heavy loads (Matthew 23:4), seeking honor for themselves (Matthew 23:5-7), and neglecting justice, mercy, and
faithfulness (Matthew 23:23). These rebukes culminate in
a lament over Jerusalem (Matthew 23:37), where Jesus
expresses His deep sorrow for their unwillingness to accept
Him.

Jesus' words here are not meant to condemn without purpose but to call out sin so that repentance might follow. His
rebuke is an act of tough love—He desires that they turn
from their ways and embrace the truth. This aligns with
Proverbs 27:5-6, which states: "Better is open rebuke than
hidden love. Wounds from a friend can be trusted, but an
enemy multiplies kisses."

Love as Fulfillment of the Law

Romans 13:10 says, "Love does no harm to a neighbor.
Therefore, love is the fulfillment of the law." Even when
Jesus pronounced woes upon the Pharisees, His ultimate
goal was not harm but correction. True love sometimes

requires confronting sin directly because ignoring wrongdoing can lead to greater harm. By exposing their hypocrisy,
Jesus was giving them an opportunity to see their errors
and repent.

Rebuking Liars Sharply

The Bible also supports sharp rebuke when necessary for
correction. For example:

- **Titus 1:13**: "This testimony is true. Therefore, rebuke
  them sharply, so that they will be sound in the faith."

- **Proverbs 19:25**: "Strike a scoffer, and the simple
  will learn prudence; reprove a man of understanding,
  and he will gain knowledge."

- **2 Timothy 4:2**: "Preach the word; be prepared in
  season and out of season; correct, rebuke and
  encourage—with great patience and careful instruc-
  tion."

These verses highlight that rebuke has its place within
Christian teaching when done with the intent of restoring
someone to righteousness.

Conclusion

Jesus' woes in Matthew Chapter 23 were not devoid of love
but were expressions of it in its most challenging form—
tough love aimed at bringing about repentance. Similarly,

Scripture supports sharp rebuke when it serves to correct falsehoods or guide others back onto the path of truth. Love does not shy away from addressing sin; instead, it seeks what is best for others by leading them toward God's truth.

Love as Fulfillment of the Law: A Life Led by the Spirit – Conclusion

The essence of love, as taught in Scripture, is not a passive or permissive emotion but an active and transformative force that fulfills the law of God. The Apostle Paul writes in Romans 13:10, "Love does no harm to a neighbor. Therefore, love is the fulfillment of the law." This profound statement encapsulates the heart of Christian living—a life led by the Spirit is one that embodies love in action, truth, and righteousness.

However, it is critical to understand that biblical love is not devoid of correction or rebuke when necessary. Jesus Himself demonstrated this balance during His earthly ministry. In Matthew 23, often referred to as "The Seven Woes," Jesus expressed righteous indignation toward the Pharisees and teachers of the law for their hypocrisy and legalism. While these words may seem harsh at first glance, they were spoken out of love—a desire to call them to repentance and lead them away from their destructive ways. Jesus' rebuke was not rooted in hatred but in a deep concern for their spiritual well-being and for those they misled.

In Titus 1:13, Paul instructs believers to "rebuke them

sharply, so that they will be sound in the faith." This direc-
tive highlights that love sometimes requires confrontation
when falsehoods or harmful behaviors threaten the integrity
of faith. Rebuking liars or those who distort God's truth is
not contrary to love; rather, it aligns with it because it seeks
to protect others from deception and guide them back to
righteousness.

A life led by the Spirit involves walking in truth (John 16:13),
which includes standing firm against sin and falsehood
while extending grace and mercy. Love does not rejoice
in wrongdoing but rejoices with the truth (1 Corinthians
13:6). Therefore, Christians are called to emulate Christ's
example—showing compassion and forgiveness while also
upholding justice and holiness.

In conclusion, love as fulfillment of the law encompasses
both tender compassion and firm correction. It seeks not
only to comfort but also to challenge individuals toward
greater conformity with God's will. As followers of Christ,
we must strive to live lives marked by Spirit-led love—love
that speaks truth boldly yet gently restores those who have
strayed from it.

Chapter 8: Abiding in Christ: Bearing Fruit of the Spirit

The concept of "abiding in Christ" is one of the central themes in the New Testament, particularly emphasized by Jesus Himself in John 15. To abide in Christ means to remain connected to Him, to draw spiritual nourishment from Him, and to live a life that reflects His character and teachings. This chapter explores what it means to abide in Christ and how doing so enables believers to bear the fruit of the Spirit as described by the Apostle Paul in Galatians 5:22-23.

The Vine and the Branches: A Relationship of Dependence

In John 15:1-8, Jesus uses the metaphor of a vine and its branches to illustrate the relationship between Himself and His followers. He declares, "I am the true vine, and my Father is the gardener" (John 15:1). In this analogy, Jesus is the source of life and sustenance for His disciples, who are represented as branches. Just as a branch cannot bear fruit unless it remains attached to the vine, believers cannot produce spiritual fruit unless they remain connected to Christ.

Jesus emphasizes this point when He says, "Remain in me, as I also remain in you. No branch can bear fruit by itself; it must remain in the vine. Neither can you bear fruit unless you remain in me" (John 15:4). The word "remain," or "abide" in some translations, signifies an ongoing relationship characterized by trust, obedience, and reliance on Christ.

What Does It Mean to Abide?

To abide in Christ involves several key aspects:

1. **Faith**: Abiding begins with faith—believing that Jesus is who He claims to be and trusting Him for salvation (John 3:16). Without faith, it is impossible to please God or maintain a relationship with Him (Hebrews 11:6).

2. **Obedience**: Jesus links abiding with obedience when He says, "If you keep my commands, you will remain in my love" (John 15:10). Obedience is not about legalistic rule-following but about aligning one's life with God's will out of love and reverence for Him.

3. **Prayer**: Abiding also involves maintaining open communication with God through prayer. Jesus encourages His disciples to ask for whatever they need while abiding in Him (John 15:7).

4. **Meditation on Scripture**: The Word of God plays a crucial role in abiding. Jesus states that His words must remain in us if we are to bear fruit (John 15:7). Regular study and meditation on Scripture help believers stay rooted in truth.

5. **Dependence on the Holy Spirit**: Abiding requires reliance on the Holy Spirit for guidance, strength, and transformation (Romans 8:9-11).

Bearing Fruit of the Spirit

When believers abide in Christ, they naturally begin to exhibit what Paul calls "the fruit of the Spirit." These qualities are listed in Galatians 5:22-23 as love, joy, peace, patience, kindness, goodness, faithfulness, gentleness, and self-control. Each attribute reflects an aspect of God's character that becomes evident in a believer's life through their union with Christ.

Love

Love is foundational because it encompasses all other fruits (1 Corinthians 13). It is selfless and sacrificial—modeled perfectly by Jesus' death on the cross (John 15:13).

Joy

Joy transcends circumstances because it is rooted not in external conditions but in one's relationship with God (Philippians 4:4).

Peace

Peace comes from trusting God's sovereignty and promises (Isaiah 26:3). It guards our hearts even amid trials (Philippians 4:7).

Patience

Patience reflects God's long-suffering nature toward humanity (2 Peter 3:9) and enables believers to endure hardships without losing hope.

Kindness & Goodness

Kindness involves showing compassion toward others (Ephesians 4:32), while goodness refers to moral integrity that seeks what is right.

Faithfulness

Faithfulness entails loyalty both toward God and others—a steadfast commitment regardless of challenges.

Gentleness

Gentleness mirrors Christ's humility (Matthew 11:29) and allows believers to respond graciously even under provocation.

Self-Control

Self-control empowers individuals to resist sinful impulses by relying on God's strength rather than their own willpower (Titus 2:11-12).

Pruning for Greater Fruitfulness

In John 15:2-3, Jesus explains that every branch bearing fruit will be pruned so it can produce even more fruit. Pruning represents God's discipline—His way of refining us through trials or challenges so we grow spiritually stronger (Hebrews 12:10-11). While pruning may be painful at times, it ultimately leads us closer into alignment with His purposes.

The Result of Abiding

The ultimate purpose behind abiding is glorifying God through fruitful living. As Jesus states clearly, "This is my Father's glory—that you bear much fruit showing yourselves disciples"(John15 :8). Fruitful lives testify powerfully in the world around them transforming communities reflecting kingdom values.

Chapter 9: Crucifying the Flesh: Victory Through Faith in Jesus

The concept of "crucifying the flesh" is a central theme in Christian theology, rooted deeply in the teachings of the Bible. It refers to the process by which believers, through faith in Jesus Christ, overcome their sinful nature and live according to the Spirit. This chapter explores the biblical foundation for crucifying the flesh and how victory over sin is achieved through faith in Jesus.

The Nature of the Flesh

In biblical terms, "the flesh" often symbolizes humanity's sinful nature—our inclination toward selfishness, rebellion against God, and indulgence in worldly desires. The Apostle Paul frequently addresses this concept in his letters. For example, in Galatians 5:19-21, Paul lists the "works of the flesh," which include sexual immorality, idolatry, jealousy, fits of anger, envy, drunkenness, and other sins. These behaviors are contrasted with the "fruit of the Spirit," which reflects a life transformed by God's power.

Paul emphasizes that those who belong to Christ have crucified the flesh with its passions and desires (Galatians 5:24). This act of crucifixion is not a literal one but a spiritual reality that occurs when a person places their faith in Jesus. By identifying with Christ's death on the cross, believers symbolically put to death their old sinful selves.

The Role of Faith in Crucifying the Flesh

Faith is essential for overcoming the power of sin and living a victorious Christian life. In Romans 6:6-7, Paul explains that our old self was crucified with Christ so that we would no longer be enslaved to sin. Through faith in Jesus' sacrificial death and resurrection, believers are set free from sin's dominion.

This freedom does not mean that Christians will never struggle with temptation or sin again. Instead, it signifies a new identity and power to resist sin through reliance on God's grace. As Paul writes in Galatians 2:20: "I have been crucified with Christ; it is no longer I who live but Christ lives in me; and the life I now live in the flesh I live by faith in the Son of God."

Faith enables believers to trust God's promises and rely on His strength rather than their own efforts. It is through this dependence on God that they can experience victory over sinful desires.

Walking by the Spirit

One practical way to crucify the flesh is by walking according to the Spirit. In Galatians 5:16-17, Paul urges believers to "walk by the Spirit" so they will not gratify the desires of their flesh. He acknowledges that there is an ongoing conflict between our sinful nature and God's Spirit within us.

Walking by the Spirit involves daily surrendering our will to God and seeking His guidance through prayer, Scripture reading, worship, and fellowship with other believers. It also requires cultivating spiritual disciplines such as self-control (a fruit of Holy Spirit) while avoiding situations or influences that may lead us into temptation.

The Power of Grace

Grace plays an integral role in enabling Christians to overcome their sinful tendencies because it provides both forgiveness for past sins as well as empowerment for righteous living moving forward (Titus 2:11-12).

Abiding in Christ: Bearing Fruit of the Spirit - Conclusion

In conclusion, abiding in Christ is not merely a passive state but an active and intentional relationship with Jesus. The Bible teaches that to bear fruit, believers must remain connected to the true vine, which is Christ Himself. As Jesus declares in John 15:4-5, "Abide in me, and I in you. As the branch cannot bear fruit by itself unless it abides in the vine, neither can you unless you abide in me. I am the vine; you are the branches. Whoever abides in me and I in him, he it is that bears much fruit, for apart from me you can do nothing." This passage underscores that spiritual fruitfulness is impossible without a deep and ongoing connection to Jesus.

The fruits of the Spirit—love, joy, peace, patience, kindness, goodness, faithfulness, gentleness, and self-control (Galatians 5:22-23)—are not products of human effort but manifestations of a life surrendered to God. These qualities reflect Christ's character and serve as evidence of His transformative work within us. By remaining rooted in Him through prayer, Scripture study, worship, and obedience to His commands (John 15:7-10), believers allow His Spirit to cultivate these virtues.

Furthermore, abiding in Christ involves pruning—a process described by Jesus in John 15:2: "Every branch that does bear fruit he prunes so that it will be even more fruitful." While pruning may involve trials or discipline (Hebrews 12:11), it ultimately leads to greater spiritual growth and maturity. It refines our character and aligns our desires with God's will.

Bearing fruit also glorifies God and fulfills our purpose as His disciples. As stated in John 15:8: "By this my Father is glorified that you bear much fruit and so prove to be my disciples." Our lives become testimonies of God's grace and power when we exhibit the fruits of the Spirit. Moreover, this fruitfulness extends beyond personal transformation—it impacts others by drawing them closer to Christ through our witness.

In light of these truths, let us commit ourselves to abide steadfastly in Christ. Let us seek His presence daily and yield to His Spirit's leading so that we may bear abundant fruit for His glory. May our lives reflect the love and holiness of our Savior as we walk faithfully with Him until we see Him face-to-face.

As Paul exhorts us in Colossians 2:6-7: "Therefore as you received Christ Jesus the Lord, so walk in him, rooted and built up in him and established in the faith...abounding in thanksgiving." Abiding is not just about receiving life from Christ but living out that life fully for His kingdom purposes.

In closing, the act of crucifying the flesh is not merely a one-time decision but an ongoing process that requires daily commitment and reliance on Jesus Christ. The Apostle Paul writes in Galatians 2:20, "I have been crucified with Christ; it is no longer I who live, but Christ lives in me; and the life which I now live in the flesh I live by faith in the Son of God, who loved me and gave Himself for me." This verse encapsulates the essence of victory over sin: it is through our union with Christ's death and resurrection that we gain power over our sinful nature.

The flesh represents our human tendencies toward sin—selfishness, pride, lust, anger, and other works of darkness (Galatians 5:19-21). However, when we place our faith in Jesus and submit to His lordship, we receive the Holy Spirit who empowers us to resist these temptations. Romans 8:13 reminds us that "if by the Spirit you put to death the deeds of the body, you will live." This means that victory over sin is not achieved through human effort alone but through walking in step with God's Spirit.

Furthermore, crucifying the flesh involves a conscious decision to reject worldly desires and align ourselves with God's will. As Paul exhorts in Galatians 5:24-25, "And those who are Christ's have crucified the flesh with its passions and desires. If we live in the Spirit, let us also walk in the Spirit." This passage underscores that true followers of Christ actively choose to deny their sinful impulses while embracing a life led by God's Spirit.

Victory through faith also brings freedom, freedom from guilt, shame, and condemnation. Romans 8:1 declares boldly: "There is therefore now no condemnation for those who are in Christ Jesus." By trusting fully in Jesus' sacrifice on the cross, believers can rest assured that their sins are forgiven and they are made new creations (2 Corinthians 5:17).

Finally, this chapter calls on readers to reflect on their own lives. Are there areas where they still struggle with sin? Are they fully surrendered to Christ's authority? The journey of crucifying the flesh may be challenging at times, but it leads to abundant life—a life marked by love, joy, peace, patience, kindness, goodness, faithfulness, gentleness, and self-control (Galatians 5:22-23). These fruits of the Spirit serve as evidence of a transformed heart and a victorious life.

Let us remember Jesus' words from Matthew 16:24-25: "If anyone desires to come after Me, let him deny himself, take up his cross daily, and follow Me. For whoever desires to save his life will lose it; but whoever loses his life for My sake will find it." True victory comes when we lay down our old selves at His feet and allow Him to reign supreme in every aspect of our lives.

As you move forward from this chapter into deeper truths about living faithfully in Christ's flesh-and-blood reality on earth as well as spiritually united with Him eternally—may you be encouraged by this promise from Philippians 4:13: "I can do all things through Christ who strengthens me."

Chapter 10: Faithful Discipleship: Known by Jesus, Not Works Alone

The concept of faithful discipleship is deeply rooted in the teachings of the Bible. It emphasizes that being a true follower of Christ is not merely about performing good works or adhering to religious rituals but about having a genuine relationship with Jesus Christ. This chapter explores the biblical foundation for this principle, drawing from key passages and teachings that highlight the importance of faith, grace, and being known by Jesus.

The Foundation of Faithful Discipleship

Faithful discipleship begins with understanding that salvation and righteousness come through faith in Jesus Christ, not through human effort or works. The Apostle Paul writes in **Ephesians 2:8-9**, "For it is by grace you have been saved, through faith—and this is not from yourselves, it is the gift of God—not by works, so that no one can boast." This passage underscores that salvation is a gift from God, received through faith alone. No amount of good deeds can earn salvation; instead, it is granted freely to those who believe in Jesus.

Jesus Himself emphasized this truth during His earthly ministry. In **John 6:28-29**, when asked by the crowd what they must do to perform the works of God, Jesus replied, "The work of God is this: to believe in the one he has sent." Here, Jesus redirects their focus from external actions to an internal posture of faith and trust in Him as the Messiah.

Being Known by Jesus

One of the most sobering teachings about discipleship comes from **Matthew 7:21-23**, where Jesus says:

"Not everyone who says to me, 'Lord, Lord,' will enter the kingdom of heaven, but only the one who does the will of my Father who is in heaven. Many will say to me on that day, 'Lord, Lord, did we not prophesy in your name and in your name drive out demons and, in your name, perform many miracles?' Then I will tell them plainly, I never knew you. Away from me, you evildoers!'"

This passage reveals that even those who perform miraculous works in Jesus' name may be rejected if they lack a true relationship with Him. The key criterion for entering the kingdom of heaven is not merely doing impressive deeds but being known by Jesus. To be "known" by Him implies an intimate relationship characterized by love, obedience, and faith.

In **John 10:14**, Jesus describes Himself as the Good Shepherd who knows His sheep and whose sheep know Him: "I am the good shepherd; I know my sheep and my sheep know me." This mutual knowledge between Christ and His followers forms the essence of faithful discipleship. It goes beyond superficial religiosity to a deep connection rooted in trust and surrender.

Faith Versus Works

While good works are not the basis for salvation or discipleship, they are evidence of genuine faith. James writes in **James 2:17**, "Faith by itself, if it is not accompanied by action, is dead." True faith naturally produces fruit—acts of love and service that reflect Christ's character. However, these works are not performed to earn God's favor but as a response to His grace.

Jesus illustrates this principle in **John 15:5**, where He says: "I am the vine; you are the branches. If you remain in me and I in you, you will bear much fruit; apart from me you can do nothing." The imagery of abiding in Christ highlights that fruitful living stems from remaining connected to Him through faith. Without this connection, any attempt at good works becomes futile.

The Role of Grace

Grace plays a central role in faithful discipleship because it reminds believers that their standing before God depends entirely on His unmerited favor rather than their own efforts. Paul writes in **Romans 11:6**, "And if by grace, then it cannot be based on works; if it were, grace would no longer be grace." This verse reinforces that salvation and discipleship are gifts received through God's initiative.

Grace also empowers believers to live faithfully as disciples. In **Titus 2:11-12**, Paul explains that "the grace of God has appeared that offers salvation to all people. It teaches us to say 'No' to ungodliness and worldly passions and to live self-controlled, upright and godly lives in this present age." Grace not only saves but also transforms believers into faithful followers who reflect Christ's character.

Obedience as Evidence of Faithful Discipleship

While faithful discipleship begins with faith and grace rather than works alone, obedience remains an essential aspect of following Christ. In **John 14:15**, Jesus declares: "If you love me, keep my commands." Obedience flows naturally from love for Christ—it is not a burdensome duty but a joyful response to His love.

The Great Commission recorded in **Matthew 28:19-20** further emphasizes obedience as part of discipleship:

"Therefore, go and make disciples of all nations, baptizing them in the name of the Father and of the Son and of the Holy Spirit, and teaching them to obey everything I have commanded you."

Here again we see that faithful discipleship involves both receiving Christ's teachings through faith (being baptized) and living them out through obedience (teaching others).

Faithful Discipleship: Known by Jesus, Not Works Alone – Conclusion

In conclusion, faithful discipleship is not measured by the magnitude of our works or the external rituals we perform but by the depth of our relationship with Jesus Christ. The Bible teaches us that salvation and righteousness come through faith in Him alone, as emphasized in Ephesians 2:8-9: "For it is by grace you have been saved, through faith—and this is not from yourselves, it is the gift of God—not by works, so that no one can boast."[1] This truth underscores that our identity as disciples is rooted in being known by Jesus rather than striving to earn His favor through deeds.

Jesus Himself declared in Matthew 7:21-23 that not everyone who calls Him "Lord" will enter the kingdom of heaven but only those who do the will of His Father. He warns against relying on outward acts such as prophesying, casting out demons, or performing miracles if they are disconnected from a genuine relationship with Him. This passage reminds us that being "known" by Jesus requires living in obedience to His teachings and walking in intimate fellowship with Him.

Faithful discipleship involves surrendering our lives to Christ and allowing His Spirit to transform us from within. Galatians 2:20 encapsulates this beautifully: "I have been crucified with Christ, and I no longer live, but Christ lives in me. The life I now live in the body, I live by faith in the Son of God, who loved me and gave himself for me."[2] As we abide in Him daily through prayer, studying Scripture, and yielding to His guidance, our lives will naturally bear fruit that reflects His character—love, joy, peace, patience, kindness, goodness, faithfulness, gentleness, and self-control (Galatians 5:22-23).[3]

Ultimately, faithful discipleship is about aligning our hearts with God's will and trusting fully in His grace. While good works are an important expression of our faith (James 2:17), they are not the foundation of our salvation or identity as followers of Christ. Instead, they flow out of a heart transformed by His love and empowered by His Spirit.

As we strive to be faithful disciples known by Jesus rather than relying on works alone for validation or acceptance before God's throne (Romans 3:28), let us remember these words from John 15:5: "I am the vine; you are the branches. If you remain in me and I in you, you will bear much fruit; apart from me you can do nothing."[4] May this truth inspire us to remain steadfastly connected to Him as we journey together toward eternity.

Chapter 11: The Power of Grace: Living Beyond Legalism and Sinful Desires

Grace is one of the most profound and transformative themes in the Bible. It is through grace that believers are freed from the constraints of legalism and empowered to overcome sinful desires. This chapter explores how grace, as revealed in Scripture, enables Christians to live a life that transcends both the rigid demands of the law and the destructive pull of sin.

Understanding Grace: A Gift, Not Earned

The Bible teaches that grace is an unmerited favor from God. In Ephesians 2:8-9, Paul writes, "For it is by grace you have been saved, through faith—and this is not from yourselves, it is the gift of God—not by works, so that no one can boast." This passage underscores that salvation cannot be earned through human effort or adherence to the law; it is a divine gift freely given to those who believe in Jesus Christ.

Legalism, on the other hand, focuses on strict adherence to rules and regulations as a means of achieving righteousness. While the law serves an important purpose—revealing sin and pointing humanity toward its need for a Savior (Romans 3:20)—it cannot save. Romans 6:14 declares, "For sin shall no longer be your master, because you are not under the law, but under grace." This verse highlights a fundamental shift for believers: they are no longer bound by the law's demands but are instead governed by God's grace.

Grace Empowers Holiness

One common misconception about grace is that it gives license to sin. However, Paul addresses this directly in Romans 6:1-2: "What shall we say then? Shall we go on sinning so that grace may increase? By no means! We are those who have died to sin; how can we live in it any longer?" Far from encouraging sinful behavior, grace empowers believers to live holy lives. It transforms hearts and minds, enabling individuals to desire what pleases God rather than what satisfies their fleshly cravings.

Titus 2:11-12 further explains this transformative power of grace: "For the grace of God has appeared that offers salvation to all people. It teaches us to say 'No' to ungodliness and worldly passions, and to live self-controlled, upright and godly lives in this present age." Here we see that grace not only saves but also instructs—it trains believers in righteousness and equips them to resist temptation.

Freedom From Legalism

Legalism often leads to spiritual bondage because it places an impossible burden on individuals. Jesus confronted this issue during His earthly ministry when He criticized the Pharisees for their hypocritical emphasis on outward compliance with religious rules while neglecting matters of the heart (Matthew 23:23-28). In contrast, Jesus invites His followers into a relationship based on love and trust rather than fear and obligation.

In Galatians 5:1-4, Paul warns against returning to legalistic practices after experiencing freedom in Christ: "It is for freedom that Christ has set us free. Stand firm, then, and do not let yourselves be burdened again by a yoke of slavery... You who are trying to be justified by the law have been alienated from Christ; you have fallen away from grace." These verses emphasize that reliance on legalism undermines one's relationship with Christ because it shifts focus away from His finished work on the cross.

Instead of striving for perfection through human effort or ritual observance, believers are called to rest in God's grace. Hebrews 4:16 encourages Christians to "approach God's throne of grace with confidence" so they may receive mercy and find help in times of need. This invitation reflects God's desire for intimacy with His children—a relationship built on trust rather than performance.

Overcoming Sinful Desires Through Grace

Sinful desires stem from humanity's fallen nature—a condition inherited from Adam (Romans 5:12). While these desires remain present even after conversion (Galatians 5:17), they no longer hold dominion over those who belong to Christ (Romans 6:6-7). Through union with Him in His death and resurrection (Romans 6:4), believers receive new life characterized by victory over sin.

Grace plays a crucial role in this victory because it redirects affections toward God rather than self-centered pursuits. As Colossians 3:1-2 advises believers who have been raised with Christ should "set [their] hearts on things above" where He reigns supreme instead focusing earthly things which often fuel sinful tendencies.

In conclusion, the power of grace is the cornerstone of living a life that transcends both legalism and the pull of sinful desires. The Bible teaches us that salvation is not earned through works or adherence to the law but is a gift from God, freely given through faith in Jesus Christ. As Ephesians 2:8-9 states, "For it is by grace you have been saved, through faith—and this is not from yourselves, it is the gift of God—not by works, so that no one can boast."[1] This profound truth liberates believers from the bondage of trying to earn righteousness through human effort.

Grace empowers us to live in freedom while also calling us to holiness. Romans 6:14 reminds us, "For sin shall no longer be your master, because you are not under the law, but under grace."[2] This means that while we are no longer condemned by the law, we are also not free to indulge in sin. Instead, grace transforms our hearts and minds so that we desire to live in obedience to God out of love and gratitude rather than fear or obligation.

Moreover, grace equips us with the strength to overcome sinful desires. Titus 2:11-12 explains, "For the grace of God has appeared that offers salvation to all people. It teaches us to say 'No' to ungodliness and worldly passions, and to live self-controlled, upright and godly lives in this present age."[3] Through grace, we are empowered by the Holy Spirit to resist temptation and pursue a life that reflects Christ's character.

Finally, living beyond legalism means embracing a relation-ship with God rather than adhering to a set of rules. Jesus Himself criticized the Pharisees for their legalistic approach to religion (Matthew 23:23-28), emphasizing instead the importance of justice, mercy, and faithfulness.[4] By focusing on these principles and relying on God's grace, we can experience true freedom—a life marked by joy, peace, and purpose as we walk in step with His Spirit.

In summary, God's grace is not only sufficient for our sal-vation but also for our sanctification. It frees us from both legalism and sin's grip while empowering us to live lives that glorify Him. As Paul wrote in 2 Corinthians 12:9: "But he said to me, 'My grace is sufficient for you, for my pow-er is made perfect in weakness.' Therefore I will boast all the more gladly about my weaknesses so that Christ's power may rest on me."[5] Let us therefore embrace this transformative power of grace as we seek to honor God in every aspect of our lives.

Chapter 12: Eternal Life Through Faith: The Promise of God's Presence

The concept of eternal life is one of the most profound and central promises found in the Bible. It is not merely an extension of earthly existence but a transformative reality that reflects the fullness of God's presence and His ultimate plan for humanity. Eternal life, as revealed in Scripture, is deeply intertwined with faith in Jesus Christ, who is described as "the way, the truth, and the life" (John 14:6). This chapter explores the biblical foundation for eternal life through faith, emphasizing its significance as a gift from God and its implications for believers.

The Nature of Eternal Life

Eternal life is often misunderstood as simply living forever. However, the Bible presents it as much more than endless existence. In John 17:3, Jesus defines eternal life by saying, "Now this is eternal life: that they know you, the only true God, and Jesus Christ, whom you have sent." Here, eternal life is described not just in terms of duration but as a relationship—a deep and intimate knowledge of God. This relational aspect underscores that eternal life begins not after death but at the moment one places their faith in Christ.

The Apostle Paul echoes this understanding in Romans 6:23 when he writes, "For the wages of sin is death, but the gift of God is eternal life in Christ Jesus our Lord." Eternal life is presented as a divine gift rather than something earned through human effort. It stands in stark contrast to death—the natural consequence of sin—and highlights God's grace and mercy toward humanity.

Faith as the Key to Eternal Life

Throughout Scripture, faith is consistently portrayed as the means by which individuals receive eternal life. In John 3:16, perhaps one of the most well-known verses in the Bible, Jesus declares, "For God so loved the world that he gave his one and only Son, that whoever believes in him shall not perish but have eternal life." This verse encapsulates the Gospel message: God's love for humanity led Him to offer His Son as a sacrifice for sin so that those who believe might be saved.

Belief or faith involves more than intellectual assent; it requires trust and reliance on Jesus Christ as Savior and Lord. In Ephesians 2:8-9, Paul emphasizes that salvation—and by extension eternal life—is "by grace...through faith," underscoring that it is not based on works but on God's unmerited favor.

The Role of Jesus Christ

Jesus' role in securing eternal life cannot be overstated. He describes Himself as "the bread of life" (John 6:35) and promises that "whoever comes to me will never go hungry, and whoever believes in me will never be thirsty." These metaphors illustrate how Jesus satisfies spiritual hunger and thirst—needs that can only be met through a relationship with Him.

Moreover, Jesus' resurrection serves as both a guarantee and a foretaste of eternal life for believers. In John 11:25-26, He proclaims to Martha before raising Lazarus from the dead: "I am the resurrection and the life. The one who believes in me will live, even though they die; and whoever lives by believing in me will never die." By conquering death through His own resurrection (1 Corinthians 15), Jesus assures believers that they too will share in His victory over death.

Living with Eternity in View

While eternal life begins at conversion when an individual places their faith in Christ (John 5:24), its full realization awaits believers after physical death or at Christ's return. This future hope profoundly shapes how Christians live today. Paul encourages believers to set their minds on things above rather than earthly concerns because their ultimate citizenship lies in heaven (Philippians 3:20-21; Colossians 3:1-4).

This perspective fosters perseverance amid trials since present sufferings are temporary compared to future glory (Romans 8:18). It also motivates holy living because those who hope for Christ's return purify themselves just as He is pure (1 John 3:2-3).

Finally—and perhaps most importantly—the promise of eternal life assures believers that they will dwell forever with God Himself. Revelation 21 paints a breathtaking picture where there will be no more pain or sorrow because "God's dwelling place [will be] among His people" (Revelation 21:3-4). This intimate communion with God fulfills humanity's deepest longing—to know Him fully even as we are fully known (1 Corinthians 13:12).

Conclusion: The Assurance of Eternal Life

The promise of eternal life is one of the most profound and hope-filled truths found in Scripture. It is not earned by human effort or merit but is freely given by God to those who place their faith in His Son, Jesus Christ. As the Apostle Paul writes in **Ephesians 2:8-9**, "For it is by grace you have been saved, through faith—and this is not from yourselves, it is the gift of God—not by works, so that no one can boast." This underscores that salvation and eternal life are acts of divine grace, accessible only through faith.

Jesus Himself assures us of this promise in **John 3:16**, saying, "For God so loved the world that He gave His one and only Son, that whoever believes in Him shall not perish but have eternal life." This verse encapsulates the heart of the Gospel: God's love for humanity and His desire for all to be reconciled to Him through belief in Christ. Eternal life begins not only after death but also here and now as we enter into a relationship with God through faith.

The Bible also teaches that eternal life is more than just an unending existence; it is about being in the presence of God forever. In **Revelation 21:3-4**, John describes a vision of eternity where "God's dwelling place is now among the people, and He will dwell with them. They will be His people, and God Himself will be with them and be their God. 'He will wipe every tear from their eyes. There will be no more death' or mourning or crying or pain, for the old order of things has passed away." This passage paints a picture of ultimate restoration—a future where sin, suffering, and separation from God are no more.

Furthermore, Jesus emphasizes that knowing Him personally is at the core of eternal life. In **John 17:3**, He prays to the Father, saying, "Now this is eternal life: that they know You, the only true God, and Jesus Christ, whom You have sent." Eternal life involves an intimate relationship with God—a deep knowledge and communion with Him made possible through Christ's sacrifice on the cross.

Believers can rest assured in this promise because it is grounded in God's unchanging character and faithfulness. As stated in **1 John 5:11-13**, "And this is the testimony: God has given us eternal life, and this life is in His Son. Whoever has the Son has life; whoever does not have the Son of God does not have life. I write these things to you who believe in the name of the Son of God so that you may know that you have eternal life." These verses provide confidence that those who trust in Jesus can know—beyond any doubt—that they possess eternal life.

In conclusion, eternal life through faith represents both a present reality and a future hope for all who believe in Jesus Christ. It assures us of God's abiding presence now and forevermore. As we live out our faith daily—walking by His Spirit (Galatians 5:25), bearing fruit for His glory (John 15:5), and persevering until we see Him face-to-face (1 Corinthians 13:12)—we cling to His promise that nothing can separate us from His love (Romans 8:38-39). This glorious truth inspires worship, gratitude, and unwavering hope as we await our ultimate homecoming with our Creator.

The Conclusion of "Faithful in Flesh: Living the True Gospel"

In conclusion, the message of the true Gospel is one that calls for unwavering faith in Jesus Christ, who came in the flesh to redeem humanity. The life and teachings of Jesus reveal that salvation is not achieved through human effort or adherence to external rituals but through a deep, personal relationship with Him. As it is written in Ephesians 2:8-9, "For by grace you have been saved through faith, and this is not your own doing; it is the gift of God, not a result of works, so that no one may boast."

Living faithfully in the flesh means acknowledging Jesus as Lord and Savior and allowing His Spirit to guide every aspect of our lives. It requires us to walk by faith and not by sight (2 Corinthians 5:7), trusting in God's promises even when circumstances seem uncertain. This faith must be active, manifesting itself in love, obedience, and a commitment to living out the values of the Kingdom of God.

The Bible teaches that what truly defiles a person is not what enters their body but what comes from their heart (Mark 7:15). Therefore, our focus should be on cultivating hearts that are pure and aligned with God's will. By doing so, we reflect the character of Christ and bear fruit that glorifies God.

As followers of Jesus, we are called to live as His ambassadors on earth (2 Corinthians 5:20), sharing His love and truth with others. This mission requires us to remain steadfast in our faith, even in the face of trials and opposition. The Apostle Paul reminds us in Romans 8:38-39 that nothing can separate us from the love of God in Christ Jesus our Lord.

Ultimately, living faithfully in the flesh means embracing our identity as children of God and walking in the freedom that comes from knowing Him. It is a journey marked by grace, empowered by the Holy Spirit, and directed toward eternal life with our Creator.

May this book serve as a guide and encouragement for all who seek to live out their faith authentically and wholeheartedly. Let us remember the words of Hebrews 12:1-2: "Let us run with perseverance the race marked out for us, fixing our eyes on Jesus, the pioneer and perfecter of faith." In Him alone do we find true hope, purpose, and salvation.

To God be all glory forevermore. Amen.

Conclusion Prayer for the Book: "Faithful in Flesh: Living the True Gospel"

Heavenly Father,
We come before You with hearts full of gratitude for the gift of Your Son, Jesus Christ, who came in the flesh to dwell among us and redeem us from sin. Thank You for revealing Your truth through Your Word and for guiding us to live

by faith, not by sight. We acknowledge that without faith, it is impossible to please You, and we humbly ask for Your strength to walk faithfully in obedience to Your will.

Lord Jesus, we thank You for Your sacrifice on the cross and for showing us what it means to live a life fully surrendered to the Father. Help us to follow in Your footsteps, denying ourselves daily and taking up our cross. May we be faithful witnesses of Your love and grace, proclaiming the true Gospel with boldness and humility.

Holy Spirit, we invite You to work within us continually. Transform our hearts and minds so that we may bear fruit that glorifies God—love, joy, peace, patience, kindness, goodness, faithfulness, gentleness, and self-control. Lead us away from temptation and deliver us from evil as we strive to live lives that honor our Savior.

Father God, as this book comes to a close, let its message remain alive in our hearts. May it inspire all who read it to seek a deeper relationship with You through faith in Jesus Christ. Let every word written here point back to Your glory and truth.

We pray this prayer in the mighty name of Jesus Christ— our Lord and Savior who came in the flesh—and through whom we have eternal life. Amen.

"Now unto Him who is able to keep you from falling and present you faultless before His glorious presence with great joy—to the only wise God our Savior be glory and majesty, dominion and power both now and forevermore." (Jude 1:24-25)

Amen.

About Apostle Bill Amor

Apostle Bill Amor's life is a testament to the power of faith, perseverance, and divine intervention. Diagnosed with autism as a child and considered high-functioning as an adult, Apostle Amor has faced challenges that would have broken many. Born into a world that often misunderstood him, young Bill struggled with feelings of isolation and inadequacy. Despite these challenges, he displayed remarkable determination. At the age of 12, he achieved a significant milestone by winning a reading competition—an accomplishment that filled him with pride and optimism.

However, this joy was short-lived when his mother tearfully shared devastating news from the doctor: he was not expected to live beyond the age of 28 to 32. This revelation shattered his world. Overwhelmed by fear and hopelessness, Bill sought solace in his best friend John Straw, only to discover that John had been taken away by his brother Andy. Feeling abandoned and consumed by anger, he fled into the woods near his home. It was there, amidst the trees and shadows of doubt, that he cried out to God in desperation. Bill's life changed forever on that fateful day. As he climbed a steep hill toward his neighbor's house, he encountered what can only be described as a divine vision: Jesus Christ Himself appeared before him at the top of the hill near a chain-link fence. The image was vivid—Jesus stood before him with pockmarks where His beard had been removed and glistening divots on His cheeks and chin. He did not resemble traditional depictions; instead, He appeared timeless yet distinct from modern trends.

This miraculous encounter marked the beginning of Apostle Amor's transformation. From a young boy who felt lost and unworthy, he grew into a man devoted to spreading God's message of love and repentance. Through trials and tribulations—including struggles with literacy—he found strength in faith and discovered his purpose as an apostle.

Apostle Amor's mission is clear: to guide others toward spiritual healing by sharing his testimony of divine grace. With humility born from hardship and wisdom gained through faith, he invites readers to embark on their own journeys toward repentance and renewal.

Apostle Bill Amor, a follower (not sent by people or through people, but by Jesus Christ—the Savior—and God the Father, who raised Him from the dead), and all those reborn in the Spirit of Jesus—the few predestined and chosen fathers, mothers, brothers, and sisters with me:

To the few chosen born-again members of Christ's Body (and we pray—not for worldly churches that follow human rules and love this wicked world; we leave them alone):

Grace and peace—calmness and spiritual health—to you from God our Father and the Lord Jesus Christ, who gave Himself to cleanse us from our sins...to save us and purify us from all unrighteousness...so He might rescue us from this evil age, according to the will and plan of our God and Father. To Him be ALL glory forever and ever. Amen.

Believers, the good news we proclaim is not a human invention. It is not derived from people, nor was it taught to us by anyone; instead, it was revealed directly by Jesus Christ, who lives eternally in His risen body.

I am astonished and deeply troubled that some of you are so quickly deserting Him who called you by the grace of Christ for a different gospel—though there is no other true gospel. There are some who are troubling you and twisting the gospel of Christ into something false. But even if we or an angel from heaven should preach a gospel contrary to what we originally proclaimed to you, let them be accursed! As I have said before, I now repeat: If anyone preaches a gospel different from what you received from us, let them be accursed!

I thank You, Father, Lord of heaven and earth, for hiding these truths from the so-called wise and learned, and revealing them to the humble and childlike. Yes, Father, for this was Your good pleasure. ▨▨

In the beginning was the Word, and the Word was with God, and the Word was God. He was with God in the beginning. Through Him all things were made; without Him nothing was made that has been made.

In Him was life, and that life was the light of all mankind. The light shines in the darkness, but the darkness has not understood it.

He came to His own people, but His own did not receive Him. Yet to all who did receive Him, to those who believed in His name, He gave the right to become children of God—children born not of natural descent, nor of human decision or a husband's will, but born of God's Spirit.

We call on you today because Jesus sent us to proclaim: You must be born again! You must be born again! For those who are born again are invited to go deeper into resting fully in Him and relying on His grace.

Jesus desires to give you a fresh start today—a new beginning. Today is your opportunity! You've heard this message before:

"For God so loved the world that He gave His one and only Son, that whoever believes in Him shall not perish but have eternal life."

Those who believe this truth embrace eternal life and enter Heaven...but those who reject it or hesitate turn away from their rescue into God's Kingdom. They resist His invitation and choose their own path toward eternal separation—Hell—an everlasting loss.

Ultimately, it comes down to your choice: God will not judge you based on your deeds alone but will ask one question: "What did you do with My Son Jesus Christ?"

Jesus Himself declared: "Come to Me, all you who are weary and burdened, and I will give you rest." (Matthew 11:28)

Jesus desires to lift you from wherever you are and bring you into His Kingdom, offering a life filled with purpose here on Earth and eternal joy in Heaven!

This is about experiencing the fullness of life now and the promise of eternal life forever.

Your time on Earth is fleeting—a mere moment compared to eternity. Choose today whom you will follow! Come to Jesus now; today is your opportunity to be saved from condemnation and shame.

You cannot change the past, and tomorrow is uncertain. But today is the day for salvation. Act now while there's still time.

Life is fragile—we've all seen people here one moment and gone the next. Don't wait until it's too late.

Call on the name of Jesus Christ today while the door remains open. There is no other name under heaven or on Earth by which we can be saved but the name of Jesus Christ.

Call on Him today, and may God bless you abundantly!

Apostle Bill Amor